L.

KELVIN C. BIAS

ARCHIVE
ZERO

ARCHIVE ZERO | NEW YORK | 2020
www.archivezero.com

Published by Archive Zero, LLC

Paperback ISBN: 978-1-7346603-7-1
E-book ISBN: 978-1-7346603-6-4

© 2020 by Kelvin C. Bias

Cover design by Robson Garcia Jr.
Formatting by Polgarus Studio.

This poetic work is based on true historic events.

INTRODUCTION

MAY 13, 2020

7:07 a.m.

It's just another day. Just another day of worrying about my family, worrying about the state of the world, worrying about finding a job, worrying about fevers and tantrums and remote learning, wondering what I will do for the next 50 years, *if* I live that long.

Today, I turn 50 years old.

I am so grateful to be here. I was born to a 15-year-old Mexican-American girl at Community Hospital in Glendora, California at 4:06 p.m.—also a Wednesday, May 13. I could have been aborted.

Sheltering in place during a pandemic is not how I expected to celebrate 50 years on this planet. No party on the French Riviera during the Cannes Film Festival. Those celluloid dreams are fun, but in the grand scheme of things, they aren't really that important. And it pains me to say, they never were. Yes, cultural events like an international film festival are important in some sense, but not in the overarching thematic sense. People all over the world are dying.

I will celebrate the little things this year, and hope and pray for a better future, for my family, for my friends, for the world. What have I truly accomplished in 50 years? Which begs another question. Is it important?

Welcome to *L.*

Kelvin C. Bias, Publisher, Poet, Philosopher

for the angels

CONTENTS

"Life is most delightful when it is on the downward slope, but has not yet reached the abrupt decline."—Seneca

L.

NULLA PRIUS. 1969

September, I don't remember.
I don't even exist.
I'm waiting to breathe
The succulence of Earth.
Two kids, on a bus,
Pomona: the
L.A. County Fair.
Conception there.
I'll see you all soon.
I've defeated chance.

NULLA. 1970

Kathleen, Alfred, Jackie, Kelvin.
Baby boy: Paredes.
The names that mean so much.
An image of a woman with black hair.
A long hall, a birth into it all.
On the third day I dream.
I adopt Mom & Dad.
I am a Bias. Thank the Lord.

I. 1971

It's official. July.
I learn to walk,
Ten-month sky.
Smiling faces.
New friends, family.
A small heart,
I also learn to bleed.

II. 1972

Lakers 33-game win streak.
I was a fan of purple and gold
Before I knew what color was.
My win streak is beginning.
West, the Logo, first title,
I still have Mom & Dad
All to myself.

III. 1973

December, front page
Of the *Los Angeles Times*.
My brother, Chris,
I wonder why they took
His photo. A black man,
With an Afro,
Holding who they
Think is a white kid
On his knee.
"A blithe spirit"
We are now four.

IV. 1974

Hong Kong Phooey.
No. 1 Super Guy.
Dad and his boys.
Son *Numero Dos* poops in the
Hallway corner,
Disregarding
His diaper and any
Attempt to flee.
Sports are far away.
Platform shoes are in.
Nixon is out!

V. 1975

Cousins and people.
Brown like me.
I don't know when
They told me I was
Adopted but it must
Have already happened.
I've always known.
"We didn't want someone
Running up to you and
Saying you're not really
My cousin."
This never occurs.
Instead, Brian and
His biological
Blonde Afro arrive.

VI. 1976

Bicentennial birthday.
Taken away when
I bit my Montessori
Teacher and crush.
Fireworks a plenty.
I still remember
Their names.
I believe everything
I am told. Innocence
Clinging to rosy
Cheeks like a fly
In a hurricane.

VII. 1977

L.A. to Niagara.
I am the navigator,
Somewhere near
Holland, Michigan.
Camp Miniwanca.
Road trip to end
Them all. Three boys
In the back of a car.
Counting license plates
And infinite horizons.

VIII. 1978

Yankees beat the
Dodgers again,
World Series.
Southern California
Doesn't know flurries.
Gasoline and strawberries
Picked from fertile fields.
GEMCO and Travel Town.
First stage smog alert.
Light pollution.
I can't see many stars
But I know
They're there.

IX. 1979

We. Are. Family.
My two brothers,
Mom & Dad, me.
We are not
Pittsburgh Pirates.
We are rapscallions,
Breaking into cabinets.
We are torpedoes,
Sinking battleships.
We are looking for
Santa Claus out
The window even
Though we know
The jig is up.

X. 1980

"You're a decade old today."
Mom's celebratory declaration
Discovered in my
Brown paper bag lunch
Next to a PB & J sandwich.
May 13: A Tuesday this year.
Three days after the
Giant Tinkertoy Incident.
The birth of stitches and a scar,
Giving hospital directions
To Cousin Cynthia
While Mom & Dad
Take Las Vegas
And Magic & Kareem
Get their ring.

XI. 1981

Bradbury, Asimov,
Arthur C. Clarke.
Devouring books
And breaking
Alarm clocks.
I remember the
Day Reagan
Got shot.

XII. 1982

The King of Pop
Thrilled,
Lakers win again,
Denise Wong tells
Me I look like
Jamaal Wilkes.
Spain, Copa Mundial.
Shame on Austria
And West Germany.
Just "Beat It".
Nonetheless,
Goals are always
Better in Spanish.

XIII. 1983

Soccer, track,
Guiding a path,
Poppin' and lockin':
I can't break dance like
The cool kids in black.
Personal computers,
Typewriters, words
On a blank page.
I write my first poem
In seventh grade English.

XIV. 1984

Orwellian weekend at McLaren.
It didn't fuck with my head.
Wrong kid in the wrong place.
I didn't know my way home.
Midnight arrival: disorientation.
It's closed now. Downtown court.
Free tickets to the Olympics.
How do you like them Apples?

XV. 1985

Memorial Day Massacre.
Not again.
Two games later,
Favor returned.
The Fabulous Forum.
Lakers finally do it.
Red don't care.
He's smoking his cigar
While Magic smiles
Ear-to-ear
And I hurdle hurdles
Reciting lines from
The Breakfast Club.

XVI. 1986

Challenger Blue.
Mr. Stanley's class.
Biological clocks.
Too bad it's an
All-boys Catholic school.
A shy athlete and girls
Don't combine well.
Unless you can
Get courtside near Jack.

XVII. 1987

Doors on stalls!
The campaign slogan
For the ages.
Someone ruined it
For everybody.
Had to do your
Business in the open.
Avulsion fracture
Healing, hurdles of
Life looming.
Quit football. Taco hell.

XVIII. 1988

Party hearty,
Surf and date.
We're the Class of '88.
Disneyland summer.
Next stop, Thumper.
Huntington Beach
Riding waves,
City or state?
SAT complete.
Admittance
Long accepted.
Mom & Dad
Porch perched.
First time on my own.
Tucson freshman.
120 degrees.
In the shade.
I almost got laid
In a midnight fountain.
Welcome to Arizona.

XIX. 1989

1989! Not another
Runner. Boot camp.
Asphalt grinder, no
Disneyland summer.
After NCAA hoop
Dreams dashed
In Denver and roadside
Freeze near Las Vegas,
New Mexico. It wasn't
A foul. Never. Again.
Volunteer. Yourself.
You appreciate
Your freedom.

XX. 1990

Back on campus.
A wild Wildcat at
The Wildcat House.
"Fuck the dumb shit."
How did we survive?
Walked upon on
The football team.
Cannon fodder
For the first platoon.
But at least we
Held out hope.
Fall leaves, girls,
Saguaros don't
Bend in the breeze.
You're a Kappa.

XXI. 1991

Palindrome year.
The beginning and the end.
Disneyland summers
Continue. Next stop
Thumper. Mickey & me.
College quest continues.
I'm still a virgin.
How can I catch HIV?
Magic can't die.
That gridiron fall,
I actually get in the game.

XXII. 1992

January euphoria.
Norwegian *au pere*
In Dad's pickup truck.
Scandinavia wasn't on
My radar. International
Intrigue ingrained
After a night at
The Red Onion.
Deserts swarm. From
Tucson to L.A.
I walk with new air
As I write what I see.
I'm a member of
The fourth estate.
I ambulate but
Do not graduate.

XXIII. 1993

Times in L.A. fall
Off the tree.
Branches growing east.
Pacific beaches
Further away.
First stop Dallas.
My life in a foreign
Country: Texas.
Enemy territory
For a Forty-Niner.
Hollywood dreams
Dormant in stride,
Blinded by the
Friday Night Lights.

XXIV. 1994

European sojourn.
Lagos, the Algarve,
A beautiful,
Bed-hopping
Finnish girl.
Madrid. Atocha.
When O.J. ran.
Paris. June 20, 1994.
Atop Gustave's gem.
Chance meeting.
Chance of a
Come-undone future.
Blinded, not by justice.
Texas tumbleweed.
College friends.

XXV. 1995

New York City
Horizon.
Five-day criss-
Cross, cross-country
Odyssey.
White Sands,
L.A., Vegas.
Tennessee,
Texas, a rear-view
Mirror. Verrazano
Approach. Brooklyn-
Bound new arrival.
Sports Illustrated,
A child's wall,
A collagist's dream.

XXVI. 1996

Fugee in a New city.
Brooklyn kid,
Listening alone in a
Dark room.
Looking for a place
In the world.
Bright fish in a
Brighter ocean.
Neon liberty.
How long will it last?

XXVII. 1997

Where to begin?
Did she actually happen?
Starter marriage, Tartars,
Barbarians at the Gate.
New York to Las Vegas
And nowhere in between.
Dancing fantasies of a future,
A monster in the making:
Return of the Mack.

XXVIII. 1998

A rumbling, an awakening,
No more Mr. Nice Guy.
I am who I am, but the power
Of not-giving-a-fuck rises,
Unearthed like a buried egg.
New York City, my yolk,
The rich protein I need.
An unlevel playing field.
New view, new friends,
Girl-chasing fiend. Nights on
The rain-slicked streets.
Spy Bar at 3:30 a.m.,
Strolling in like what.

XXIX. 1999

Y2K, party over?

No, no, no.

Summer in Paris.

Love at the top

Of the Eiffel Tower.

Seriously? Not again.

A brief window of ecstasy

Unfurled at Gustave's

Point of amorous energy.

My power zone, an eternal pier.

I hope it can power my fallow

Future, my libidinous desert.

Energy cannot be destroyed.

Tears don't exist in the past.

Enjoy it while it lasts.

Making love in Italy,

Spilling iodine on a Roman bed.

Prince lives.

He'll never die.

I don't need a little red corvette

To have some fun,

And I'm already crazy.

What will I remember in 21 years?

Does it matter?

XXX. 2000

Zero, zero, zero.
I am still here.
When I was
A young boy
Steeped in the 1970s,
Thirty was a distant age,
A milestone too far away
To comprehend.
I thought I would
Die when I turned 30.
But instead I witness:
The hanging chad,
The birth of the
Lies of Mass Destruction,
The Lakers back where
They belong, threepeat
In the making, Tokyo,
Hong Kong, love in the
Afternoons, evenings,
Morning walks of shame.
We are all still here.
Some in memory,
Others flesh and blood.
I hope the world
Stays on its axis,
And I don't fall off.
I dream the
Indestructible Dream.

XXXI. 2001

Lost in a haze of NYC nights
Until the terrible happens.
I was hungover in New Jersey.
Thought it was a joke.
I had vomited from
Too much debauchery,
Hours earlier in the
Moonlight shadow of
The Towers. Wee light.
Not the best look
For a horrific morning.
That part I'd like to forget.

XXXII. 2002

Another palindrome year.
Trips, tripped up.
I did selfish things.
I'm sorry.
I hold remorse.
A bad state of mind
Dissipates eventually.
No condition to be in a relationship.
I'm still a work-in-progress
Because stubborn is my pipe.

XXXIII. 2003

I did not squander my youth.
Fun is fun.
"Good writing fodder."
If nothing else,
There is forever a
Stormy august summer,
Punctuated by an
August night.
"Are you going to get in?"
I assumed nothing,
But clearly wanted.
Imagine what almost
Couldn't have been.
I'll always cherish this memory,
The lasting grin it brings.
Yet time marches on.

XXXIV. 2004

I am a blur of decadent
Late-night behavior
That I'll view as "nostalgia"
Later when I can't replicate
It's masterful disregard for
Responsible financial living.

Dubya stays in.
Ohio does not save a nation.
It lays more sinister plans
For a historic future.
Blue states *and* red states.
Are we United?

XXXV. 2005

Curly, curly, curly.
No hair, but a song.
And a beautiful girl.
If I hadn't noticed
The cat jumping,
Where would we be?
Cannes, again,
This time with a film.
Dreams and art.
It's a start.

XXXVI. 2006

Burning, yearning.
I tumble. I face rebukes.
Twisted like a pretzel,
Growing pains from
An upended way of life.
Good things come
From those we wait for.
Escalate the noble,
Forgive the cruel.
Keep my mouth shut.

XXXVII. 2007

No longer a single man.
All Saint's Day.
Parents and reception.
Hearts aligned.
Through flights and fights,
Missives, don't quit.
Angels will arrive.
Angels we will love and know.

XXXVIII. 2008

Crashed. Belly up,
But for hope, hope,
Hope! Obama!
Yes, we can.
We can and will.
We've made it a year.

XXXIX. 2009

Enter the Void.
Another May,
Another Cannes.
The *Croisette*
Of life wide open.
Unwashed dishes
Don't cause fights.
Plights, fleeting.

XL. 2010

A new decade. Forty.
What's the difference?
I feel none. The world
Doesn't care anyway.
It remains hard,
A tectonic plate
Beneath my feet,
Drifting through time.
One, two, three.
Post-production,
A man of action/inaction,
Depending on who you ask.
We're not done.

XLI. 2011

The days wax and wane.
I can take a walk
Because I can.
First and last film
In the can.
My last trip to Cannes.
Sleep walking is a
Thing of the past,
Manhattan nights,
Seldom more.

XLII. 2012

The words don't have to be
Perfect. Let them linger,
Marinate in melancholy.
What happens in New York,
Stays in New York.
We're floating.
Icebergs unmelted,
In need of some
Global warming.
Iceland calls.
Black sand and elasticity.
Hold on. Time is your reward.
Angels are on the horizon.

XLIII. 2013

They say you become
A man when your father dies.
Maybe I just made this up.
I remember the last July weekend,
Cleaning up the garage,
Going through my found scribblings,
Dad nudging me in the direction
I had taken a detour from,
Beyond the cardboard boxes,
The old rap cassettes,
Public Enemy, Heavy D,
M.C. Hammer, gathering dust,
The rising, root-buoyed asphalt,
The land that remained while
He stood in the driveway with Mom,
One last time as I drove away.

XLIV. 2014

Trying in Moscow the
Previous fall. We still
Await the angel's arrival.
In January, conception,
The best-ever perspiration.
A few months later,
We squealed when we
Learned the first angel
Was a girl. We wanted to
Know before. Prepare.
We are an excited lot,
Watching bicycle kicks
On a tiny monitor.
Wiggleworm: Oct. 22,
Eyes looking up, shining.
We never knew such joy.
We *knew* we had
All the love in the world.

XLV. 2015

Parenthood: Year One
In the books. Nine-month
Walker, keeping us
On our toes, immense
Feelings tip the scales
Toward the future,
Guardian eyes
Filled with happiness.
Curious fingers
Reaching for knowledge.

XLVI. 2016

A dark cloud, bloviating,
Approaches. I inure
Myself to the coming
Carnage, viral vitriol,
By collapsing inward.
Family is important.
Grow, learn, play.
A future for our nation.
A future for our Union.
A precious daughter,
Will soon have a sister.
Our cup runneth over.

XLVII. 2017

February morning.
The moment of
Second truth,
The junior angel
Arrives on a 23-degree
Morning. The next day:
No. 1 visits No. 2.
The apprehensive look,
The wonder, the awe,
Sister calms sister down.
The sublime road.
We are now four.

XLVIII. 2018

Thailand in January.
We travel so free,
Maskless, unbound,
Halfway around the
World, and a day.
Sparkles and bubbles,
Parks and playpens.
From the city to the sea.
Coney Island glee.
Our global, summer, endeavor.

XLIX. 2019

Life hums a proud tune:
Defiant, stubborn, free.
A pantry, lines of goods,
Not lines of the
Unemployed. We
Remain in a sacred bubble.
Numb to the mass shootings,
The cresting waves, the tide
Of unfiltered hate,
As long as we can buy food.
We take trains in Japan.
Ignorant of the American
Problem. The "isms" rising.
Girls 1 and 2. They play,
And we learn from their
Unbridled magic.

L. 2020

Love, love, love, love, love.
If I write the word enough,
Will it transform this horrible year?
Now we all get to wear a mask,
To hide our true feelings,
To quell hate, to quell romance?
To move on, pack lies like
Gutter balls, shoot them,
Again and again and again?
Flood waters of freedom.

No, no, no, no, no.
We must rinse the hate.
Wash our thoughts in
Healing action.
I write to bridge gaps,
To open my heart,
To work, to try to improve.
My wife, our daughters.
We, together, loving in place.
We are always home.

ACKNOWLEDGMENTS

First and foremost, thank you to my family. Thank you, Mom and Dad and my brothers. And thank you to many, many others: Robson Garcia, Chilembwe Mason; James Chan, Hiromi Saeki, Chi Mac, Faisal Azam, Erica Velis, John Plenge, Paul Gutierrez, Dimitry Léger, Naomi Castillo, Lisa Darling, Karen Lee, Ancel Bowlin, Caryn Prime, Scott Hevesy, Jaramay Aref, Richard Demak, Larry Mondi, Joy Birdsong, Natasha Simon, Susan Szeliga, Karen Meneghin, Diane Smith, Gabe Miller, John Shostrom, Pam Roberts, Kevin Kerr, Tony Scheitinger, Jill Jaroff, Nancy Ramsey, Bernice Rohret, Joan Rosinsky, Anne Vallersnes, Sonja Kiefer, Bettina Meetz, Linda Bukasen, Julia Luu, João Serejo, Kevin Gidden, Claudia Ancalmo (and everyone from Disneyland), Karen Strauss, Brian Jaramillo, Cynthia Cortes, Jennymar, Mrs. Pell, Lars Anderson, Tracy Mothershed, Simone Procas, Judy Margolin, Gary Garrison, Andrea Woo, Albert Chen, Bob Der, Jordan Bell (and everyone at Stitcher), Lisa P. LeGrand, Andrew Paredes, Jackie Bergman, Mike Johnson, Leslie Bornstein, Julian Rozzell Jr., the cast and crew of all my independent films, Seevon Chau and family, Marina and Jason Anderson of Polgarus Studio, everyone at the Minskoff Theater, everyone at St. Matthias, The Bias Family, The Pitts Family, The Smith Family, The Takahashi Family, The Tanaka Family, The Lao Arpasuwong Family, our Brooklyn friends and neighbors, The Cervantes Family; The Sigur Family and everyone on Light Street; Willie Joe Philbin and The Philbin Family, my friends, fraternity brothers and football teammates at the University of Arizona, my classmates at NYU. If I have forgotten anyone, it was not intentional. Everyone has helped me on my 50-year journey. Thank you to anyone who has ever written, read or listened to a poem, and to those of you who are thinking about it. I hope you enjoy this latest collection. Thank you the reader, the watcher, the seeker, the human being…the angels.

Kelvin C. Bias, New York City, December 2020

OTHER WORK BY KELVIN C. BIAS

MILKMAN (Novel)

What happens when everyman Calder Boyd starts to lactate? The Manhattanite becomes a media cause célèbre nicknamed the Milkman and old and new problems spill forth. The son of a former NBA star and a Norwegian artist, Calder copes with his strained marriage, losing his copywriting job at a boutique ad agency, a male-empowerment espousing mailman and a porn-star performance artist who wants to exploit him. He also deals with his late father's legacy and his wife's past indiscretion—all while breastfeeding their newborn daughter. Calder eventually becomes a pawn in the battle between a feminist organization and a militant men's society as he tries to become a better husband and man. The Fourth Estate, sex, art, love, memory, marriage and family converge during the snowiest winter on record in this commentary on contemporary American fatherhood.

WHISPERS OF A DYING SUN (Poetry)

These poems represent the vestiges of man from the perspective of a distant future. Akin to radio signals, the remnants of humanity streak toward a black hole where art, politics, love, technology, philosophy, science and the yearning for eternity accrete. Prophetic, stoic, polyphasic, the words disassemble and recombine on the other side in search of a new sun. I hope these poems find a closer home in your personal universe, heard but you're unsure of their origin, like whispers.

SEXOPOLIS: POEMS ON LOVE AND SEX

Love is a liberation, an act, a rebellion, a restriction, a communion. This poetry collection covers the universal topics of love and sex. From erotic to platonic and from marital to familial, love comes in many forms. We don't always get it, but we all crave it.

IMMACULATE DUST: LOVE POEMS

This poetry collection delves headlong into the world of love. Encompassing the realms of dream, fantasy and reality, the poems intend to engender not just love, but more pointedly, lovemaking. Lust. Love. Languor. These are three states of mind and body before, during and after the most pleasant poetry of human interaction: consented sex. We all possess desire and we are all made of dust. Immaculate dust.

21 PARTICLES OF ETERNITY (Poetry)

Is eternity a quantifiable entity? An existence that can be divided into smaller particles, assembled and disassembled like a puzzle? Can it be bent? Borrowed? Recycled? Eternity is elusive. It constantly seems beyond our grasp yet always within our reach. *21 Particles of Eternity* covers topics as disparate as Mars and pornography, and ranging from global warming and parenthood to politics and death. The poet posits this: perhaps there are hidden portals where eternity can be glimpsed for fleeting moments, and the quest to find them brings meaning. How many particles will you find?

IF THE SKY IS AWAKE (Poetry)

Why do we have a 24-hour day, 60-minute hour, and 60-second minute? Thank the ancient Egyptians, Sumerians and Babylonians. Going further back, in humanity's early days, time was simply measured by the interval between sunrise and sunset. Today, we have much more precise methods. One second is defined as the duration of 9,192,631,770 periods of the radiation corresponding to the transition between the two hyperfine levels of the ground state of a cesium 133 atom. Confusing? Yes. Sometimes what transpires in daylight is the purest. Each day is a new dawn, a chance to reinvent yourself, find new love, rekindle an old one, and peer into the sky and feel awake. Reading poetry is like living life by your own clock. Lose yourself in your own sky.

THE LAST WILL & TESTAMENT OF THE UNITED STATES OF AMERICA: POETRY

This poetry collection conveys my anger and sadness over the current state of America—black, brown, yellow, red, white, and blue. On May 25, 2020—Memorial Day—a white woman named Amy Cooper walked her dog without a required leash in an area of Central Park known as the Ramble, and Christian Cooper, a peaceful, bird-watching black man, asked her to leash her dog. The legacy of slavery writ-large in the astounding fact they had the same surname. Amy responded by calling 911 to say that "an African-American man" was threatening her and her dog. Christian calmly recorded the incident. (Imagine what might have happened if he hadn't.) The video went viral and provided a painful reminder of the tradition of white women falsely accusing black men of a crime. Later that night, in Minneapolis, Minnesota, a black man named George Floyd, who was not resisting arrest, was pressed face down into the pavement with a knee to his neck for eight minutes—eight minutes—by white Minneapolis police officer Derek Chauvin. Floyd died as he narrated his own death. "I can't breathe." Protests over Floyd's killing raged in cities across America for days, weeks…forever? On July 17, John Lewis, civil rights icon and Georgia Congressman, died from pancreatic cancer, and a few days before he passed, he wrote an essay to be released on the day of his funeral. On July 30, it ran in *The New York Times*. In his essay, Lewis wrote: "When you see something that is not right, you must say something. You must do something." *The Last Will & Testament of the United States of America* is the poet's way of saying and doing "something."

ABOUT THE AUTHOR

Kelvin C. Bias is a journalist, novelist, poet, filmmaker, and raconteur. However, his most important moniker is father. He holds a B.A. in Political Science from the University of Arizona and an M.F.A in Screenwriting from NYU. He lives in New York City with his family.

L. is his seventh poetry collection. Connect with Kelvin on Instagram: @kelvincbias